CONTENT

MICHAEL JORDAN	1
LEBRON JAMES	8
KOBE BRYANT	14
LARRY BIRD	21
STEPHEN CURRY	28
ALLEN IVERSON	34
SHAQUILLE O'NEAL	41
KEVIN DURANT	47
TIM DUNCAN	53
DERRICK ROSE	59

Michael Jordan: The Flight of an Icon

Prologue: A Legacy of Excellence

Michael Jordan's journey in basketball is more than just a tale of athletic prowess; it's a story of resilience, dedication, and a relentless pursuit of greatness. His legacy transcends the sport, embodying the essence of what it means to strive for and achieve excellence.

Chapter 1: Early Challenges and the Fuel for Greatness

Michael Jordan's childhood in Wilmington, North Carolina, laid the foundation for his legendary basketball career. Facing the pivotal challenge of being cut from his high school varsity basketball team as a sophomore, Jordan experienced a significant emotional and motivational turning point. Rather than letting this setback defeat him, he channeled his disappointment into a fierce determination to improve.

Jordan's response to this early adversity was to intensify his training regimen. He played on the junior varsity team, where he quickly became a standout player, honing his skills and gaining the confidence that would propel him to varsity success.

This experience taught him the value of hard work, perseverance, and turning failure into fuel for success. His subsequent rise to become a star on the varsity team laid the groundwork for his future achievements and demonstrated his resilience and relentless pursuit of excellence.

Chapter 2: Collegiate Success and the Birth of a Legend

At the University of North Carolina at Chapel Hill, Jordan's basketball journey continued to flourish. He made an immediate impact on the Tar Heels' program, showcasing not only his athletic prowess but also his ability to perform in high-pressure situations. His game-winning shot in the 1982 NCAA Championship game as a freshman was a defining moment, highlighting his clutch performance ability and solidifying his reputation as a rising star in basketball.

At UNC, Jordan further developed his game under the guidance of legendary coach Dean Smith. This period was instrumental in refining his skills, understanding of the game, and preparing him for the rigors of professional basketball.

His collegiate success, including numerous accolades and a consensus National College Player of the Year award, set the stage for his entry into the NBA.

Chapter 3: Redefining Greatness in the NBA

Entering the NBA as the third overall pick by the Chicago Bulls in 1984, Jordan faced the challenge of transitioning to the professional level and the pressure of high expectations. His early years in the NBA were marked by individual success but not immediate team success. Jordan responded to these challenges by pushing himself to new heights and becoming a leader on and off the court.

His relentless drive, combined with his unique talent, gradually transformed the Bulls into a formidable team. Jordan's ability to elevate the play of his teammates, coupled with his own spectacular performances, turned the Bulls into a championship-caliber team. His competitive nature and dedication to winning were pivotal in overcoming obstacles and achieving team success.

Chapter 4: Triumph, Retirement, and Comebacks

Jordan's career with the Bulls was marked by unprecedented success, including six NBA championships and numerous MVP awards. However, his journey was interspersed with personal challenges, including the tragic loss of his father and two retirements from basketball. His first retirement in 1993 to pursue a career in baseball, a tribute to his late father's dream, showed his multifaceted talent and resilience in facing personal grief.

Jordan's return to the NBA in 1995 marked one of the most celebrated comebacks in sports history. He led the Bulls to three more championships in a second three-peat, re-establishing his dominance in the sport. His second comeback with the Washington Wizards after his second retirement further demonstrated his enduring passion for basketball and his ability to compete at the highest level despite advancing age and changing team dynamics.

Michael Jordan's story is a remarkable narrative of overcoming adversity, relentless pursuit of excellence, and unparalleled success.

His legacy extends beyond his athletic achievements, embodying the spirit of resilience, hard work, and the relentless pursuit of greatnes.

Epilogue: More Than an Athlete

Beyond his on-court achievements, Jordan's impact extends to his business ventures, philanthropy, and influence on popular culture. His brand, Air Jordan, revolutionized sports marketing, and his commitment to giving back is evident in his numerous charitable endeavors.

Quotes Section:

On Failure: "I've missed more than 9,000 shots in my career. I've lost almost 300 games. Twenty-six times, I've been trusted to take the game-winning shot and missed. I've failed over and over and over again in my life. And that is why I succeed."

On Perseverance: "Obstacles don't have to stop you. If you run into a wall, don't turn around and give up. Figure out how to climb it, go through it, or work around it."

On Success: "Talent wins games, but teamwork and intelligence win championships."

On Self-Belief: "You must expect great things of yourself before you can do them."

LeBron James: A Journey from Hardship to Heights of Greatness

Prologue: A Story of Determination and Triumph

LeBron James' ascent in the world of basketball is not just a story of unmatched athleticism and skill. It's a saga of overcoming life's hurdles, relentless determination, and an unwavering commitment to excellence. His journey from the streets of Akron, Ohio, to becoming one of the greatest basketball players in history is a tale that continues to inspire and motivate.

Chapter 1: Challenging Beginnings

LeBron James' journey began in Akron, Ohio, where he was born into a life filled with uncertainty and hardship. Raised by his single mother, Gloria, in often precarious living conditions, LeBron experienced the struggles of poverty firsthand. This challenging environment, however, did not dampen his spirit. Instead, it fueled his ambition and desire to rise above his circumstances.

From a young age, basketball served as LeBron's escape and a source of joy amidst adversity. He recognized early on that his talent on the court could be his ticket to a better life.

At St. Vincent-St. Mary High School, LeBron's extraordinary abilities became evident. His high school career was nothing short of phenomenal, marked by spectacular performances and significant media attention. LeBron's dedication to improving his game, coupled with his physical gifts, made him a standout athlete, and he quickly became a national sensation.

Chapter 2: Rising to Fame

LeBron's leap from high school phenom to NBA superstar was both highly anticipated and fraught with immense pressure. Selected first overall in the 2003 NBA Draft by the Cleveland Cavaliers, he was thrust into the spotlight as the face of a franchise and the hope of a city. This transition, daunting for any teenager, was met by LeBron with a level of maturity and composure that belied his years.

In the NBA, LeBron quickly dispelled any doubts about his ability to compete at the highest level. His impact on the game was immediate and transformative.

LeBron's blend of size, athleticism, and basketball IQ allowed him to dominate on both ends of the court. He redefined the forward position, bringing a unique combination of power and finesse that the league had seldom seen.

Chapter 3: Achieving NBA Greatness

LeBron's career, spanning stints with the Cleveland Cavaliers, Miami Heat, and Los Angeles Lakers, has been a journey marked by extraordinary achievements and accolades. He has earned multiple NBA championships, MVP awards, and All-Star selections, each milestone a testament to his relentless pursuit of success.

However, LeBron's path was not without its share of obstacles. He faced intense scrutiny and criticism, particularly during his move to Miami and his subsequent return to Cleveland. LeBron's ability to handle this pressure, to use criticism as motivation, and to remain focused on his goals is a key aspect of his legacy. His resilience, particularly in bouncing back from defeats and challenging seasons, has been a hallmark of his career.

LeBron's journey is more than a story of athletic success; it's a narrative of overcoming adversity, embracing challenges, and relentlessly pursuing greatness. His evolution from a high school prodigy to a global basketball icon is a testament to the power of hard work, resilience, and a steadfast belief in one's abilities.

Chapter 4: Beyond Basketball

LeBron's influence extends beyond the basketball court. He is a philanthropist, activist, and a role model. His commitment to giving back to his community, particularly to the city of Akron, is evident through initiatives like the "I Promise School," aimed at supporting at-risk children.

Epilogue: A Living Legend's Legacy

LeBron James' legacy in basketball and his contributions to society are monumental. His journey from hardship to the heights of basketball greatness is a vivid illustration of the power of dreams, hard work, and perseverance.

Quotes Section:

On Overcoming Challenges: "I think, team first. It allows me to succeed, it allows my team to succeed."

On Determination: "You have to be able to accept failure to get better."

On Leadership: "I always say, decisions I make, I live with them. There's always ways you can correct them or ways you can do them better. At the end of the day, I live with them."

On Success: "I like criticism. It makes you strong."

KOBE BRYANT

14

Kobe Bryant: The Mamba Mentality

Prologue: A Legend's Journey
Kobe Bryant's journey in the world of basketball is a tale of extraordinary talent, unmatched work ethic, and a relentless pursuit of greatness. Known for his "Mamba Mentality," Kobe's story is one of overcoming challenges, constant self-improvement, and achieving legendary status in the NBA.

Chapter 1: Early Years and Love for Basketball
Born on August 23, 1978, in Philadelphia, Pennsylvania, Kobe Bryant was introduced to basketball at a young age. His father, Joe Bryant, a former NBA player, was a significant influence. Kobe spent some of his early years in Italy, where his father played professionally. This unique experience broadened Kobe's perspective on the game and fueled his passion for basketball.

Chapter 2: High School Stardom and NBA Leap
After returning to the United States, Kobe Bryant attended Lower Merion High School in Pennsylvania. There, he quickly rose to prominence as a basketball prodigy. His high school career was nothing short of spectacular, characterized by breathtaking performances and a remarkable ability to dominate games. Kobe led Lower Merion to a state championship, showcasing not just his scoring ability but also his leadership and competitive fire.

Despite his high school success, Kobe's decision to bypass college basketball and jump straight to the NBA was seen as audacious and risky. At the time, few players had made a successful transition directly from high school to the professional league. This leap posed significant challenges for Kobe, as it meant competing against seasoned athletes with more experience and physical maturity.

Chapter 3: Rise to NBA Greatness

Drafted 13th overall by the Charlotte Hornets in the 1996 NBA Draft and then traded to the Los Angeles Lakers, Kobe faced a daunting challenge: the transition from high school basketball to the NBA's rigors. Kobe's early years in the league were a mix of exhilarating highs and challenging lows. He had to adapt to the physicality of the game, the complexity of professional plays, and the mental aspect of competing at the highest level.

Kobe's response to these challenges was marked by an intense work ethic and an insatiable desire to improve. He spent countless hours training, refining his skills, and studying the game. Kobe's dedication quickly paid off, as he began to display the brilliance that would define his career. His ability to learn from his experiences and adapt his play style was critical in his evolution into one of the NBA's elite players.

Chapter 4: Championships, Challenges, and Resilience

Kobe's tenure with the Lakers was a journey of both personal and professional growth.

He led the team to five NBA championships, establishing himself as one of the greatest players in the history of the sport. However, his path was not without its trials. Kobe faced numerous challenges, including significant injuries that tested his physical limits and resilience.

Additionally, Kobe navigated complex team dynamics and high expectations, both from himself and the fans. His ability to overcome these challenges was a testament to his mental toughness and the "Mamba Mentality" he embodied. This philosophy, characterized by fierce determination, constant learning, and a refusal to give up, became the cornerstone of Kobe's approach to life and basketball.

Kobe Bryant's story from a high school sensation to an NBA legend is a compelling narrative of overcoming adversity through relentless dedication, constant self-improvement, and an unwavering competitive spirit. His legacy extends beyond his achievements on the court, inspiring athletes and individuals worldwide to embrace challenges and relentlessly pursue their goals.

Epilogue: Legacy of a Legend

Kobe Bryant's untimely passing in January 2020 left a profound impact on the world of sports and beyond. His legacy extends far beyond his achievements on the court. Kobe was a mentor, an inspiration to young athletes, and a dedicated family man. His dedication to his post-basketball career, including winning an Academy Award, and his philanthropic efforts showed the depth of his character and passion for making a difference.

Quotes Section:

On Perseverance: "The most important thing is to try and inspire people so that they can be great at whatever they want to do."
On Hard Work: "I can't relate to lazy people. We don't speak the same language. I don't understand you. I don't want to understand you."
On Overcoming Challenges: "Everything negative - pressure, challenges - is all an opportunity for me to rise."
On Determination: "If you're afraid to fail, then you're probably going to fail."

LARRY BIRD

Larry Bird: The Legend from French Lick

Prologue: A Tale of Grit and Greatness
Larry Bird's story in the NBA is one of unwavering determination, exceptional skill, and a relentless drive to excel. His journey from the small town of French Lick, Indiana, to becoming one of basketball's greatest players is a testament to the power of hard work, resilience, and the pursuit of excellence.

Chapter 1: Humble Beginnings
Larry Bird's early life in the small towns of West Baden Springs and French Lick in Indiana was marked by economic hardship and personal struggles. Growing up in a poor family, Bird experienced firsthand the challenges that come with financial instability. These early experiences were not just hurdles; they shaped his resilient character and instilled in him an unwavering determination to rise above his circumstances.

Bird found solace and purpose in basketball, a sport that quickly turned from a pastime into a passion. The local courts became his sanctuary, a place where he could hone his skills and escape the difficulties of his daily life. Bird's dedication to the game was extraordinary.

He would spend hours practicing, often alone, working on every aspect of his game. His commitment was fueled not just by a desire to escape poverty, but by a genuine love for the game.

Despite his evident talent, Bird's journey was not smooth. He initially struggled to gain recognition, playing in a high school and an area not known for producing basketball talents. This lack of early exposure made his path to basketball stardom more challenging but also more rewarding.

Chapter 2: Collegiate Success and a Storied Rivalry

Bird's basketball journey took a significant turn when he attended Indiana State University. Here, Bird not only showcased his talent but also transformed the Sycamores into a formidable team. His college career was marked by phenomenal performances, leading Indiana State to an NCAA Championship game appearance.

It was during his collegiate years that Bird's rivalry with Magic Johnson began, a rivalry that would go on to become one of the most storied in basketball history. This rivalry pushed Bird to elevate his game further, showcasing his competitive spirit and desire to excel against the best.

Chapter 3: Dominance in the NBA
When Bird entered the NBA, drafted by the Boston Celtics in 1978, he was stepping into a league dominated by athleticism and physicality. Bird, with his unassuming appearance and lack of explosive athleticism, faced skepticism. However, he quickly dispelled any doubts about his abilities.

Bird's impact on the Celtics and the NBA was immediate and profound. His playing style – marked by exceptional shooting, basketball intelligence, and an ability to read the game – changed how a forward played the game. He led the Celtics to multiple NBA championships, reigniting the franchise's storied legacy and igniting a fierce rivalry with the Los Angeles Lakers, fronted by Magic Johnson.

Chapter 4: Overcoming Challenges and Cementing a Legacy

Bird's career, though illustrious, was not devoid of challenges. He faced several injuries that threatened to derail his playing days. Each injury was a setback, but Bird approached his recovery with the same determination and hard work that he applied on the court. He adapted his playstyle to cope with these physical limitations, ensuring that his influence on the game remained undiminished.

Larry Bird's journey from a small town in Indiana to the pinnacle of basketball greatness is a narrative of overcoming adversity, relentless hard work, and an unwavering commitment to excellence. His story continues to inspire not just athletes but anyone facing challenges, proving that with dedication and resilience, one can rise to the top and leave an indelible mark.

Epilogue: More Than Just a Player

Larry Bird's legacy extends beyond his on-court achievements. He is remembered for his leadership, his fierce competitiveness, and his contribution to the revival of the Celtics' dynasty. After his playing days, Bird continued to impact the game as a successful coach and executive.

Quotes Section:

On Hard Work: "I've got a theory that if you give 100% all of the time, somehow things will work out in the end."

On Winning: "A winner is someone who recognizes his God-given talents, works his tail off to develop them into skills, and uses these skills to accomplish his goals."

On Overcoming Adversity: "I wasn't real quick, and I wasn't real strong. Some guys will just take off and it's like, whoa. So I beat them with my mind and my fundamentals."

On Success: "Push yourself again and again. Don't give an inch until the final buzzer sounds."

Stephen Curry: The Underdog Who Revolutionized Basketball

Prologue: Defying Expectations
Stephen Curry's journey to NBA superstardom is a story of shattering expectations and redefining the possibilities of basketball. Known for his extraordinary shooting ability and his transformative impact on the game, Curry's path to success is a testament to perseverance, innovation, and the power of self-belief.

Chapter 1: Humble Beginnings
Stephen Curry's entry into the world of basketball was shaped by his unique family background. Being the son of Dell Curry, a respected NBA player, meant that basketball was a significant part of his life from the beginning. However, Stephen's path was not paved with the usual expectations of legacy. His physical stature and perceived lack of athleticism brought skepticism about his potential in professional basketball.

During his high school years, Curry's slender build was often seen as a disadvantage, leading many scouts and coaches to underestimate his abilities on the court.

This lack of recognition from elite college programs was a significant hurdle. However, Curry's passion for the game and his determination to succeed pushed him to work harder. He focused on honing his skills, particularly his shooting and ball handling, turning his perceived weaknesses into strengths.

Chapter 2: Overcoming Collegiate Obstacles
Curry's collegiate journey at Davidson College was marked by his relentless pursuit to prove his doubters wrong. As a player at a smaller, lesser-known basketball program, he faced the challenge of getting noticed. Curry rose to the occasion spectacularly, leading Davidson on an astonishing NCAA tournament run that captured the nation's attention.

His extraordinary shooting range and high basketball IQ were on full display, making him a standout player. Despite his success at Davidson, skepticism persisted about how his game would translate to the NBA. Curry's response to these doubts was to continue refining his skills, focusing on his unique strengths and preparing himself for the challenges of the professional game.

Chapter 3: Rise to NBA Stardom

Drafted seventh overall by the Golden State Warriors in 2009, Curry entered the NBA with much to prove. His early years in the league were not without challenges. He faced significant injuries that raised questions about his durability as a professional player. These setbacks could have derailed his career, but Curry's resilience shone through.

Dedicated to becoming one of the best, Curry committed himself to a rigorous training and conditioning program. He worked tirelessly to strengthen his body and refine his playing style. This hard work paid off as he not only overcame his injury struggles but also started to change the landscape of the NBA. Curry's exceptional three-point shooting and playmaking abilities challenged traditional basketball strategies and defenses, leading to a transformative impact on how the game is played.

Stephen Curry's journey from being underestimated due to his physical stature to becoming an NBA superstar and revolutionizing basketball is a narrative of relentless hard work, self-belief, and resilience.

His story is a powerful example of how perceived limitations can be turned into groundbreaking strengths, inspiring a generation of players and fans alike.

Chapter 4: Champion and Innovator
Curry's impact on the NBA is profound. He became the face of the Warriors' dynasty, leading them to multiple championships and earning several MVP awards. His ability to shoot from long range stretched defenses like never before, changing the strategic approach to the game across the league.

Epilogue: An Inspirational Figure
Stephen Curry's legacy goes beyond his on-court achievements. He is a role model for aspiring athletes, showing that skill, creativity, and intelligence can overcome physical limitations.

Quotes Section:

On Self-Belief: "Success is not an accident, success is actually a choice."
On Perseverance: "I can get better. I haven't reached my ceiling yet on how well I can shoot the basketball."
On Overcoming Doubts: "Be the best version of yourself in anything you do. You don't have to live anybody else's story."
On Work Ethic: "I'd rather be a non-All-Star playing in the Western Conference Finals than an All-Star who's sitting at home in May."

ALLEN IVERSON

Allen Iverson: The Journey of Resilience and Grit
Prologue: Defying the Odds

Allen Iverson's story in the world of basketball is a powerful testament to overcoming adversity and embracing one's unique talents. Known for his incredible skill, tenacity, and influence on the culture of the sport, Iverson's journey from a challenging childhood to becoming an NBA icon is filled with lessons of resilience and determination.

Chapter 1: Overcoming a Troubled Past

Allen Iverson's journey began in the tough neighborhoods of Hampton, Virginia, where he was confronted with the harsh realities of poverty and instability. His childhood was a constant battle against the challenges that often accompany economic hardship. Iverson found solace in sports, particularly basketball, where his natural talent was undeniable.

However, Iverson's path to success was nearly derailed by legal troubles during his high school years.

A highly publicized incident resulted in a controversial conviction, casting a shadow over his promising future in basketball. This period was one of the most challenging phases of Iverson's life, threatening to end his basketball aspirations prematurely.

Despite these formidable obstacles, Iverson's determination to pursue his basketball dreams remained unshaken. His conviction was eventually overturned, a pivotal moment that reignited his journey toward basketball stardom. Iverson's resilience during this tumultuous time was a testament to his inner strength and unwavering commitment to his goals.

Chapter 2: Collegiate Success and NBA Stardom

Iverson's basketball prowess led him to Georgetown University, where under Coach John Thompson's mentorship, he blossomed into a standout player. At Georgetown, Iverson honed his skills and developed a playing style that would become his signature in the professional league.

His time in college was marked by exceptional performances, showcasing his speed, agility, and scoring prowess, which set him apart from his peers.

Entering the NBA as the first overall pick in the 1996 Draft by the Philadelphia 76ers, Iverson faced the daunting task of transitioning from college to the professional league. His early years in the NBA were a mix of awe-inspiring plays and learning experiences. Iverson's confidence, coupled with his unique playing style, quickly captured the attention of fans and earned him respect within the league.

Chapter 3: Reshaping the NBA

Iverson's impact on the NBA was profound and immediate. His aggressive scoring approach, combined with extraordinary ball-handling skills, challenged the traditional norms of how the game was played. In a league often dominated by taller players, Iverson's relatively small stature was seen as a disadvantage. However, he turned this perceived weakness into his greatest strength.

His heart and competitive spirit on the court were unrivaled. Iverson led the league in scoring multiple times and was named the MVP in 2001, an honor that solidified his status as one of the game's greats. Iverson's influence extended beyond the court; he became a cultural icon, reshaping not only how the game was played but also influencing the culture around basketball.

Allen Iverson's journey from a challenging childhood to NBA superstardom is a narrative of resilience, talent, and the relentless pursuit of greatness. His story inspires many, proving that with determination and a steadfast commitment to one's goals, it is possible to overcome adversity and achieve extraordinary success.

Chapter 4: Legacy of a Fighter

Throughout his career, Iverson faced numerous challenges, including injuries and controversies. However, his resilience in the face of these obstacles only added to his legend. Iverson's authenticity, both on and off the court, resonated with fans worldwide, making him a cultural icon.

Epilogue: An Inspirational Icon

Allen Iverson's legacy in basketball extends beyond his on-court achievements. He is celebrated for his indomitable spirit, his influence on basketball culture, and his unwavering commitment to being true to himself.

Quotes Section:

On Perseverance: "The only thing that can stop me is me. And I'm not going to let me stop me."

On Hard Work: "I don't want to be Jordan, I don't want to be Bird or Isiah, I don't want to be any of those guys. I want to be Allen Iverson."

On Overcoming Challenges: "When you are not practicing, someone else is getting better."

On Resilience: "You can put a murderer in front of me, and I'm going to compete."

SHAQUILLE O'NEAL

Shaquille O'Neal: A Giant's Tale of Success

Prologue: From Challenges to Champion

Shaquille O'Neal's journey in the world of basketball is a remarkable story of overcoming obstacles and achieving greatness. Known for his dominant presence on the court and charismatic personality off it, Shaq's path from a young, tall kid facing hardships to becoming one of the most formidable players in NBA history is both inspiring and motivational.

Chapter 1: Overcoming Self-Doubt with Dedication

As a young boy, Shaquille O'Neal often felt conscious of his size and strength, attributes that set him apart from his peers. However, basketball provided him with a platform where these very attributes became his greatest assets. On the court, Shaq's towering presence and physicality were not just accepted but celebrated. Yet, it wasn't his size alone that made him a remarkable player; it was his dedication to honing his skills and understanding the nuances of the game.

Shaq recognized early on that to excel in basketball, he needed to be more than just a big player.

He worked tirelessly on his footwork, post moves, and basketball IQ, transforming himself into a well-rounded player. This commitment to improvement was evident in his play, where his agility and skills often surprised opponents who expected him to rely solely on his size.

Chapter 2: Collegiate Success and Entering the NBA

At Louisiana State University, Shaquille O'Neal quickly emerged as a dominant force. His performances for the LSU Tigers were a blend of raw power and refined basketball technique. Shaq's impact on the college game was profound, earning him numerous accolades and solidifying his reputation as a top prospect.

Entering the NBA as the first overall pick in 1992, Shaq faced the immense pressure of expectations. Transitioning from college to the professional league, he had to adapt to playing against more experienced and skilled opponents. However, Shaq's transition was seamless. His unique combination of size, athleticism, and refined skills made him an instant sensation in the league, setting the stage for a storied NBA career.

Chapter 3: Dominating the NBA and Becoming a Legend

In the NBA, Shaq redefined the center position. His ability to dominate games was unparalleled. Playing for teams like the Orlando Magic, Los Angeles Lakers, and Miami Heat, Shaq was a key player in leading his teams to multiple championships. His basketball intelligence, coupled with his physical prowess, made him one of the most feared players in the league.

However, Shaq's journey in the NBA was not without its share of challenges. Criticisms over certain aspects of his game, particularly his free-throw shooting, were persistent. Additionally, Shaq had to navigate complex team dynamics, especially during his tenure with the Lakers. Despite these challenges, Shaq's resilience and adaptability shone through. He continually worked on improving his game and adapting his playstyle to remain effective and influential on the court.

Shaquille O'Neal's journey from a self-conscious youngster to an NBA legend is a testament to the power of embracing one's unique qualities and tirelessly working to improve.

His story inspires not just athletes but anyone facing self-doubt and challenges, proving that with dedication, resilience, and the willingness to adapt, it's possible to overcome hurdles and achieve greatness.

Chapter 4: Impact Beyond Basketball
Shaq's influence extends beyond his on-court achievements. Known for his larger-than-life personality, he has been a successful entrepreneur, actor, and media personality. His philanthropic efforts and commitment to making a positive impact are as integral to his legacy as his basketball accolades.

Quotes Section

On Overcoming Challenges: "Excellence is not a singular act but a habit. You are what you do repeatedly."

On Success: "I never worry about the problem. I worry about the solution."

On Hard Work: "There is no substitute for hard work and effort beyond the call of duty. That is what strengthens the soul and conquers the mind."

On Resilience: "I'm like tax. You're going to pay one way or the other."

Kevin Durant: The Odyssey of Resilience and Excellence

Prologue: From Challenges to Championship Glory

Kevin Durant's story in the world of basketball is a narrative of resilience, exceptional talent, and an unyielding drive for success. His journey from a humble beginning to becoming one of the NBA's most prolific scorers and champions is a tale that resonates with the power of determination and hard work.

Chapter 1: Early Life and the Spark of Passion

Kevin Durant's childhood in Washington D.C. was a crucible that shaped his future greatness. Growing up in an environment with limited opportunities and resources, Durant found in basketball not just a sport, but a lifeline. It was on the local courts that he discovered a sense of purpose and a platform to express his talents.

Durant's physical attributes, particularly his unusual height for his age, made him a standout on the court. But it was his relentless work ethic and deep passion for the game that set the foundation for his future success.

Durant dedicated himself to mastering the fundamentals of basketball, often practicing for hours on end and challenging himself against older, more experienced players. This rigorous training honed his skills and forged a competitive edge that would become one of his trademarks.

Chapter 2: Collegiate Success and NBA Aspirations

Durant's journey to the University of Texas marked a turning point in his career. Here, he displayed not just his scoring prowess but also a versatility that was rare for a player of his stature. His single season with the Longhorns was a showcase of his basketball intelligence, agility, and an ability to dominate games, earning him national acclaim and the attention of NBA scouts.

The transition from college to the NBA is a formidable challenge for any player, and Durant was no exception. Chosen second overall by the Seattle SuperSonics in the 2007 NBA Draft, he stepped into the league with high expectations. His rookie season was a testament to his adaptability and skill, as he navigated the faster pace and physicality of the NBA, earning the Rookie of the Year honor and setting the stage for a remarkable career.

Chapter 3: Rising to NBA Stardom

Durant's impact on the NBA was both immediate and profound. In a league brimming with talent, he quickly established himself as one of the most versatile and formidable scorers. Durant's unique combination of height and shooting ability presented a matchup nightmare for opponents. He became a scoring champion multiple times and evolved into the cornerstone of the Oklahoma City Thunder's success.

However, Durant's path to NBA stardom was strewn with challenges. Criticism over his team's performance in crucial games and scrutiny over his personal decisions, particularly his move to the Golden State Warriors, tested his resolve. Durant faced these challenges with introspection and maturity, focusing on his growth as a player and a person. He used the criticism as fuel to improve and refine his game, ultimately leading his teams to NBA championships and earning Finals MVP awards.

Kevin Durant's journey from the playgrounds of Washington D.C. to the pinnacle of basketball success is a narrative of resilience, hard work, and an unwavering dedication to his craft.

His story is a testament to the idea that with perseverance and a steadfast commitment to improvement, any obstacle can be overcome, and the greatest of heights can be achieved.

Chapter 4: Achieving Championship Glory

Durant's pursuit of an NBA championship saw a significant turn when he joined the Golden State Warriors. His decision was met with both admiration and criticism, but Durant remained focused on his goal. With the Warriors, Durant's exceptional play was instrumental in winning back-to-back NBA championships, and he was named the NBA Finals MVP twice.

Epilogue: Beyond the Court

Kevin Durant's influence stretches beyond his basketball achievements. He is known for his philanthropic efforts, business ventures, and as a role model for aspiring athletes. Durant's journey is a testament to the power of resilience, embracing challenges, and relentlessly pursuing one's dreams.

Quotes Section

On Overcoming Challenges: "Hard work beats talent when talent fails to work hard."

On Persistence: "My style is not flashy, not huge on the entertainment side. But I am productive, and I do it every day."

On Success: "I've been second my whole life. I was the second-best player in high school. I was the second pick in the draft. I've been second in the MVP voting three times. I came in second in the Finals. I'm tired of being second... I'm done with it."

On Growth: "I'm a person that's always growing and evolving."

TIM DUNCAN

Tim Duncan: The Quiet Force of Nature

Prologue: A Legacy of Steadfast Excellence

Tim Duncan's journey in the NBA is a tale of quiet determination, consistency, and unheralded dominance. Known as "The Big Fundamental," Duncan's path from a swimmer in the Virgin Islands to one of the greatest power forwards in basketball history is a story that epitomizes the power of dedication, humility, and the pursuit of excellence.

Chapter 1: Unlikely Beginnings and a Shift in Destiny

Tim Duncan's early aspirations in the world of competitive swimming set the foundation for his disciplined approach to sports. However, the destruction of his primary training facility by Hurricane Hugo and a deep-seated fear of sharks forced him to pivot towards a different path - basketball. This transition was not seamless. Basketball was a sport Duncan initially approached with reluctance, a stark contrast to the water where he had felt most at home.

The transition from the pool to the basketball court brought its own set of challenges.

Duncan had to adapt not only to the physical demands of a completely different sport but also to a new way of training and thinking. His early days on the court were filled with trials and errors as he learned the fundamentals of basketball from scratch. However, Duncan's athletic abilities, combined with a tireless work ethic, gradually turned his raw potential into refined skill.

Chapter 2: Collegiate Growth and NBA Draft
Duncan's journey took a significant turn at Wake Forest University. It was here that his talents truly began to flourish. Under the guidance of Coach Dave Odom, Duncan developed an all-encompassing understanding of basketball. His defensive skills, coupled with a growing offensive game, made him a standout player in college basketball.

His collegiate career was marked not only by statistical achievements but also by the development of his leadership abilities and basketball intelligence. This period of growth and maturity paved the way for his entry into the NBA.

In 1997, Duncan was drafted first overall by the San Antonio Spurs, a decision that would greatly impact both the player and the franchise. Transitioning from college to the NBA is a daunting task for any player, but Duncan's approach was methodical and composed. His rookie season was marked by impressive performances, quickly earning him the NBA Rookie of the Year title and signaling the arrival of a new basketball force.

Chapter 3: Mastering the Game and Leading by Example

In the NBA, Duncan's impact was both immediate and transformative. His arrival in San Antonio marked the beginning of what would become one of the most successful eras in Spurs history. Duncan's playing style was a blend of efficiency, consistency, and an intelligent approach to the game. He redefined the power forward position, excelling in every facet of the game and becoming a model of consistency.

Despite his success, Duncan's career was not without its challenges. He had to navigate changes in team dynamics, the pressure of maintaining high performance, and physical challenges, including injuries.

His response to these obstacles was reflective of his character: steady, composed, and relentlessly focused on the betterment of his team. He adapted his game as needed, always putting the team's success above personal accolades.

Tim Duncan's journey from an aspiring swimmer to an NBA legend is a testament to adaptability, perseverance, and understated excellence. His story is an inspiration, proving that success is not just about natural talent but also about the willingness to learn, adapt, and dedicate oneself to continuous improvement. Duncan's legacy in the NBA is not only defined by his championships and individual awards but also by his leadership, his unassuming nature, and his commitment to the game.

Chapter 4: A Legacy of Humility and Greatness
Tim Duncan's influence extends beyond his on-court achievements. Known for his humility and low-key demeanor, he was a leader who led by example. His career is a testament to the power of steady, consistent excellence and the impact of quiet leadership.

Quotes Section:

On Consistency: "Good, better, best. Never let it rest. Until your good is better and your better is best."

On Leadership: "The time when there is no one there to feel sorry for you or to cheer for you is when a player is made."

On Success: "I'm just here to play basketball."

On Resilience: "You have to take the initiative and play your game. In a decisive set, confidence is the difference."

Derrick Rose: A Tale of Resilience and Redemption

Prologue: The Rise, Fall, and Rise Again
Derrick Rose's journey in the NBA is a poignant story of soaring heights, devastating setbacks, and a relentless pursuit of redemption. Known for his explosive athleticism and unwavering spirit, Rose's path from being an MVP to battling career-threatening injuries and then making a courageous comeback is a testament to his resilience and determination.

Chapter 1: Meteoric Rise to Stardom
Derrick Rose's journey began in the tough neighborhoods of Chicago, a city known for its rich basketball heritage. From a young age, Rose exhibited a natural affinity for basketball, nurtured on the courts of his community where he would play against local talent, honing his skills and developing a competitive edge. His raw talent was evident, but it was his dedication and hard work that began to shape his future in basketball.

At Simeon Career Academy, Rose blossomed into a star. He led his team to two state championships, showcasing not just his athletic ability but also his leadership and clutch performance in critical games. These high school years were not just about winning games; they were about building a foundation of discipline, teamwork, and resilience.

Rose's talent earned him a place at the University of Memphis, where he continued to excel. His time in college was marked by impressive performances that took the team to the NCAA championship game. Rose's ability to dominate games, combined with his exceptional speed and agility, made him a standout player, drawing the attention of NBA scouts and fans nationwide.

Chapter 2: Ascension to NBA Greatness
Entering the NBA as the first overall pick by the Chicago Bulls in 2008, Rose was stepping into a world of high expectations. His transition to the league was meteoric. Rose's rookie season was a showcase of his potential, earning him the NBA Rookie of the Year award.

By his third season, Rose had ascended to the pinnacle of NBA success. His electrifying play, marked by explosive speed and an uncanny ability to score, made him a fan favorite and a nightmare for defenses. In 2011, Rose's hard work and dedication culminated in him being named the NBA's Most Valuable Player, the youngest in the history of the league. He had reached the heights of individual achievement and seemed on track for a career filled with accolades and possibly championships.

Chapter 3: Battling Adversity

However, fate had other plans. Rose's career trajectory changed dramatically with a torn ACL in the 2012 playoffs, the first in a series of injuries that would challenge his career. These injuries were not just physical setbacks but also mental and emotional tests. The path to recovery was strenuous and solitary, filled with uncertainty.

The struggle to return to his pre-injury form was immense. Each injury and subsequent recovery was a battle, as Rose had to not only regain his physical strength but also rebuild his confidence on the court.

The journey was fraught with setbacks and challenges, including doubts about his future in the sport he loved.

Yet, Rose faced these challenges head-on. With determination and a relentless work ethic, he focused on his rehabilitation, committed to returning to the game. His resilience during this period was a testament to his character, showcasing a spirit that refused to be defeated by adversity.

Derrick Rose's story is one of extraordinary talent, meteoric rise, and the harsh reality of unexpected setbacks. It's a narrative that speaks to the heart of sports and life – the struggle against odds, the pain of loss, and the enduring power of the human spirit to overcome challenges. Rose's journey continues to inspire, a reminder that even in the face of adversity, with perseverance and determination, one can still strive for greatness.

Chapter 4: The Journey of Comeback

Rose's comeback in the league was a journey marked by perseverance, resilience, and a deep love for basketball.

He faced both highs and lows as he worked to regain his form, playing for several teams, including the New York Knicks, Cleveland Cavaliers, and Minnesota Timberwolves. Each step of the way, Rose's determination never waned, as he continuously worked to adapt his game and stay competitive.

Epilogue: A Symbol of Resilience

Derrick Rose's story transcends the game of basketball. It's a narrative about the human spirit's capacity to face adversity, to rise after falling, and to find strength in vulnerability. His journey continues to inspire those who face their own battles, in sports and in life.

Quotes Section: Derrick Rose's Words of Inspiration
On Resilience: "I believe that if you're doing something good, the universe will conspire to help you."
On Overcoming Adversity: "Everybody has their downfalls, but it's how you pick yourself up that really counts."
On Determination: "I'm not afraid of failing. I don't like to fail. I hate to fail. But I'm not afraid of it."
On Perseverance: "I can still play this game at a high level; I know that. But now, it's like I want to show people that I can play it at a high level."

www.ingramcontent.com/pod-product-compliance
Lightning Source LLC
LaVergne TN
LVHW021450231224
799792LV00005B/481